NOVEMBER BUTTERFLY

November Butterfly

Tania Pryputniewicz

Saddle Road Press

November Butterfly
© 2014 by Tania Pryputniewicz

Saddle Road Press
Hilo, Hawai'i
http://saddleroadpress.com

All rights reserved. No part of this book may be reproduced or transmitted in any form or by any means without written permission of the author.

Cover and author photographs by Robyn Beattie

Cover and book design by Don Mitchell

ISBN 978-0-9913952-1-7

Library of Congress Control Number: 2014941278

For my husband Mark

Contents

I

Marilyn	11
Sylvia	13
Amelia, or The Poem of Endings	16
Rose is a rose is a rose (*Sacred Emily*, Gertrude Stein)	17
For the Love of Three Oranges	18
Nabokov, clearly you are *not* to be confused	21
She dressed in a hurry	22
The Chanter's Daughter	24
Thumbelina	25
Ophelia	26
Inquisition	28
Isabelle: Beaurevoir Castle	29
Joan, 21st Century	30
Nefertiti Among Us	31
Thutmose, Court Sculptor	33
Kiya	35
Nefertiti On the Astral	36

II

Mordred's Dream: A Refusal	41
The Corridor	42
Totem	44
Veil	45
Accomplice	46
Veil II	47

Transport	48
Anniversary	51
What Sets Her Apart, Asks Jayne Reading Another Guinevere Poem for me in Massachusetts	52
What Sets Her Apart, II	53
Guinevere Braves High Noon in My Backyard	54
(25) Floors Up on Open Balcony in Seattle Guinevere Fails to Appear	55
Guinevere Sets the Record Straight	56
Guinevere, 4:33 am, San Diego, California	57

III

Someone	61
Peer Counselor	62
Dragonfly	64
Absolute Power	65
Third Planet from the Sun	67
Orion	68
November Butterfly	70
The Longing of the Species	72
Ocelli	73
God's in the butter	75
A Maritime Trilogy	76
Black Angel: Scripted, Never Shot	79
Wind God, Ghost Ranch	80
Divorce, or The Year of 11 Houses	81
A Boy Like You	83
3 a.m. Service, New Melleray Monastery	85
Acknowledgements	89
About Tania Pryputniewicz	93

I

Marilyn

Mother would say I was born
naked and blind like a hummingbird,

no bigger than a bumble bee, able to get
as much lift from down-beat

as up, unaware of danger: neither
preying mantis camouflaged below

nor kestrel by air. By far the largest
bone in my body: the breast!

to house the useless nonsense
of my heart, and a gorget

at throat, as if male,
with duplicitous shift of color

grey one moment, crystal red
the next, so strangers glanced twice

without knowing why—and, mother
complained, I came to crave

that staring, tongue feather-tipped
for wicking nectar. No girl sets out

to die, but that last cold night, I could neither
shake my slumber nor raise my heartbeat,

petals mammoth—veined and labial—
consuming my tiny, hovering head.

Sylvia

I. My stove

is white.
I think of you.
And fraylines of the beet
spun out into earth.
Is it sleep or words
you miss, or neither?
Glowflies, lemon-assed
rub dusty nethers
over clover. Purple
plums, bit quick
to the gaphole.
Tongue to pit, lick
that hairline rim of gold,
so hot, so cold.

II. Rooks, etc.

Learned men—professors I trusted—
put you on their syllabi. Crows

bordered the seams of my lover's leaving,
timed spigots of sprinklers

spattering the collards of the student gardens.
Crossing campus on a bicycle that night

in the mist without a light, I knew it futile
to follow beneath the downy egrets, undisturbed,

in the tree tops, all creatures—and him—
so deeply housed in separate worlds of kin,

muffled but solaced, like the damp echo
of Bibles snapping shut, teeth of another girl's

zipper un-notching in his hands, morning
approaching. Then, the rain in her hair and in mine,

ions in the air beginning their alignments
to the advancing storm.

III. Paltrow plays you

in someone's version of your life.
Three children of my own now,

I can no longer side with you
the way I could at twenty.

Camera's pulling up aerial, trawling
towards ceiling over crib

where your newly departed self
views your crying infants

and strangers wheeling
your draped body away. I concede:

girl poets will continue to trace the path
of your potency, the seduction

remains. I thank your husband
for burning the pages he did—sparing us

an orbit from which gravity
may not have had the strength

to deliver me back to my own, waiting
for me with empty plates at the table,

windows fogged with breath and steam
roiling up out of the pot on my stove.

Amelia, or The Poem of Endings

Blood-wing blackbird,
deserting again the nest

of spice, to burn,
in the circle of my domain:

the open miles of sky,
my body—and edges

of a stranger's forged
wings—meeting

at the cusp of dawn,
valves sweetening, a self

making its love
to the self and god

approving. Breath stirred
loose from sheets,

the smell of someone's
touch. One horizon. Two

stars. No one
listening. Except

you for you, crossing
for the crossing.

Rose is a rose is a rose (*Sacred Emily,* Gertrude Stein)

> "Six years after her death, *The Rose* was resurrected from its cocoon by the Whitney and finally displayed."—Gabrielle Selz, "Jay DeFeo's Rose Has Wings," Huffington Post

Stein cursived hers on her ceiling for Alice.
Jay DeFeo ceded hers one canvas,

eight years, two thousand pounds of paint, three names,
Deathrose, White Rose, surrender inevitable: The Rose.

To resurrect a work mummified in a basement
you'll need a team to drill core samples,

another to restore former tones. Luminaries
of science, textile, film, and a funder

to risk collateral art to raise the sleeper,
shoulder lobes of petals scored and rayed

like a moon god dropping her robe
at the cusp of DeFeo's body and yours.

For the Love of Three Oranges

(after the Italian fairytale *The Three Oranges*)

I. Before the orange

there was the well, wet bucket bottoms
over my shoulders, yoked by my older sister,
the dank pink of her unburdened heels
lifting before me on the path
while monarchs lined
the sides of the split cypress trunk
in shuddering thousands of pairs,
black rims encircling each spat of back-lit ember
neatly partitioned as the diamond portals
of the eyeless bird skull on mother's altar.
My sister cupped one in her hands. *They're mating.
Or dying,* she said. Deer, hosting ticks,
fled into the woods, silt flanks jerked still
by our voices. Between those trees I first felt it,
like dusk, or the roil of the astral body
down thumbs-width tunnel between dreams:
the dark horse-bites of men's glances.

II. From inside the orange

it was sweet—hot, rashy, a bed of pulp,
a rush of sorts, my head upright so as not to drown
in juice or fear, eyelashes fringed with sting,
witch's bargains reverberating through my brain,
but more—underneath, her rage at aging,
heels cracked; a little salve might have shorn
her cruelty. Slick pods of seeds slid coreward
in the night, creeping down silky tributaries
toward central spoke. I supped, then gagged.
I dreamt I was a cocoon, reversing its order
(no promise of wings) from girl to that miraculous
liquid state. I could have stayed—
but soon came a man who cut through the peel,
slicing my toes, anonymous as worms,
my thirst so great that when he brought water
I drank, and thus incurred my debt,
called it love, and followed him blindly home.

III. After the orange

Death's premonition came as a thin black line
skirting the gills of my mushrooms,
as just before harvest, a third day of rain
tipped the balance from that I'd eat
to that'd rot the rest, and sicken my girl. She's out
with him, hunting; he's given her a skill
at least, that'll feed her. Now I finger blouses,
which to shroud my sister in one last time.
After my husband freed me from the witch,
we saw little of my sister; she loved me enough
to stay away (they the better match),
though now she's gone I wish one more fire
to warm her by—to watch the burning:
split hearts of oak, listening to the particular singing
as the heat's offered, *better the wood than us*,
how she warned me; how like a younger sister
I disregarded her, sure it was jealousy, not love.

Nabokov, clearly you are *not* to be confused

with H.H. Or a mushroom in the woods.
Pale skirt aslant, chocolate brown undertines

moored by white pole. But what precisely *did*
you intend? Direct as Prufrock daring himself abstain

or eat his peach, or Lolita wake! from barbiturate
sleep to run, shedding notions never hers, as a nectarine

between two palms, pressed, surrenders the teardrop
of its pit. Or Sky Chief's daughter, duped, loses

to Raven, her face lit as she de-lids each box within
box to reach orb of sun, which at her father's

command she'll give away to morning birds' brash trills,
unaware like each of us which Gretl choose years later

follow us home, impelled by magnet of heart, lost
filings clinging in a crown over a breast long void of milk.

She dressed in a hurry

    (for Lady Di)

or perhaps never wore a slip. The photo
the press loved: a girl in a skirt, distance

between her thighs backlit by the sun,
a circle of children in her care birthed

by other mothers. The obvious
didn't escape him: she could bear heirs

and be advised on attire, as they headed for
the silks of coronation, duress of his mistress,

the inevitable rain, wet hull of a tunnel,
tracer arcs of the streetlamps of Paris,

the velvet interior of a limousine, rivulets
of silver traversing her window, silver

crisp inch of air she let in, lifting the bangs
off her forehead, cooling her throat,

hot lemon crepes doled into the hands
of lovers on side-streets at the moment

of impact. There should've been days
of bare feet on private lawns, time

to see her sons marry, their world no less sure
or less fraught with danger, the medics

of France advancing as she followed
a firefly into the thinning mist,

above the antiseptic green of the Eiffel grid
and over the Seine, past the boys in tights

dressed as plums, the fence of floodlights,
grey backs of fallow deer sidling

through the royal forests, slight as moths
and the slowly descending sheath

of cotton draping her knees, morning's bath
water still beading her shins.

The Chanter's Daughter

She sings for sparrows in her head. Inside each sparrow,
she storms for air, rushing the silt brown rivers
in each eye. She is shrill, a blue-bell, a bar, a hill,

a shell, a walrus on a hot rock bark barking. Eyes
of the forest embedded in planks plank her in a room: watch, watch
listening. She sings and soldiers come,

words you can't spell, the short ditch, a smell by the house, sudden tap
and shatter of breaking glass. Mother, father, brother, killed. What of
forgiveness. Give me

a mouth. Will you shave a head to find her again.
Or wear a hat in fear in the mirror, cover raw
and just born your yolk scalp, crouching gold,

coldly in the pupils of her eyes—a sparrow trapped
in a skin capped shadow, your unaware deity.
When she sings, all her edges

whiten like a frame.

Thumbelina

You never spoke of the disparity
in our size, nor mole
in my future, the snuffled grub
of his damp antlered

kiss. I weighed my options
to the cadence of earthworms
as I fled engagement—
memory of your sill

and milkweed tufts
tucked in my walnut-shell
bed a sharpish sorrow,
like the distance away

I stood when you sang
so your voice would not knock
me over. Nor did I once ask after
my father, nor question your

appetite for motherhood till now:
blind suitor, snow numbed
sparrow, and a man with wings
no taller than I the witch never

suspected I'd find. No matter:
it still ended with you, alone,
childless again at the window.

Ophelia

    (after the painting, *The Rescue of Ophelia*, by Christine DeCamp)

First over basket's rim: a handful
of strawberries, ripe cherries, meant

for him, the simple garnish of pinecones,
white petals of daisies torn

from dusty orbs of their hems. The queer
eddy of her thoughts circling possible futures

void of men, queen, court. Dark mallow
of cattails loosed idly by her thumbs.

The tug and rip of ditch weeds, stalk juice
greening finger-beds, wrists, dank clumps of dirt

clotting her toes. Buttons she kept buttoned,
ivory as her hair, until garland braided

and tip of limb beckoning. And a weakness
in the tree, some prior injury to trunk

she could not fathom she climbed
towards. Amber glint of ants, skirts

snagging on bark as she straddled
and clung, intent wholly on hanging

blossom's braid where it best could be seen
from untended terrain of acres

she played in with her brother as a child,
small salve for the shock of how quickly men

kill men. She'd pray for rain, watch it come.
Instead, the maddening snap and surge

of falling, her wide unfreckled forehead as it broke
the river's skin. Owl's blur of mother folding

her in, head resting on an embroidered pillow
bordered by the visions of nuns.

Inquisition

Were there maples, then, that spring
when the questions came and the men—

jade undersides of leaves albino
in the sun, so far from home where birds
portioned sky with foreign trills.

When did it begin—the irrepressibles
they could not stand? Your escape
from the messy particulars of love,

ruined by God and lucid dream:
the braid, red and blue,
gliding between your hips,

brine of sweat on eyelids,
curved backs of wasps feeding
on fallen fruit in your mother's yard.

It goes on still, inside certain girls:
the disintegrate spin of ecstasy,
portal to that sexless realm

that blessed you with your plan
long past their putting you to death,
each blade of grass halved and haired

against your cool, bare arches
as you answered in your head.

Isabelle: Beaurevoir Castle

I try not to think of you falling for seventy feet
without saints, a first—their failure

to appear. If not to speak, to stall your flight.
You landed knees to chest, shins stung,

spine jammed, dry moat against one hip,
amniotic silt on bitten tongue, its liver

aftertaste. A ball of gnats wimpled the sky;
two tiny spiders with milky opal abdomens

fled. You fasted three days. Then saddled
your horse, rallied your men. Why alter

your course? Neither threat of trial
nor my love enough to deter you,

umbilicus that bridged the damp blue beat
of my heart to yours no harbinger of obedience.

Joan, 21st Century

You'd consider it brutish how I observed
so quickly unconcerned my former body

burning below, zealous confirmants
raking the coals and dumping my remains

in the Seine. A peasant girl held a wooden cross
to my eyes; the crowd subsumed her

and Isabelle petitioned for years
to restore honor to my name. Even now

I'd be outcast, this century littered
with as many hidden enemies as friends,

success hinging on whose guardians
of god I angered least, stolen apples

browning along the wet edge
of my every bite.

Nefertiti Among Us

The TV's neutral male voiceover
covers what we love about Egypt

and their pharaohs: house-sized rocks
that formed the pyramids dropped in place

without machine, sentries to this day
guarding the embalmed dead, the slight

queen's beauty and betrothal to her cousin,
the nested outlined peacock rings binding

her eyes. *Someone must've hated her,*
the archeologist granted permission

to view the body cries, wiping tears
and her sheer scarf

aside, shards of her black earrings
swinging, toenails painted coral inside

the ribs of her sandals. She's the first
in a quarter of a century to have this honor,

and fears she's the last, gesturing numbly
with a dusting brush to the mummy's

lime-white face, a gash where mouth
should've been. *Who could've done this?*

she repeats from spans of sand
she crossed on camelback and foreign floors

she stood upon for hours in line to gain
access, countless midnights hunched

over hieroglyphics til they rippled away
off the page like heatwaves, til she slept

with shoulders square but shifted right, knees
to the left to match the jut of chin in sympathy.

Thutmose, Court Sculptor

She could have sent a lesser servant
or one of her five remaining daughters

but she came herself instead to view
progress of the bust, her narrow

toes and ankles silted white
from tilled furrows she crossed

on foot, consumed as I
with questions of what would

persist—*surely the pyramids—but
what of this?* I asked, cupping

her elbow, turning us to face
the sun, kissing her wrist, silver

plaited threads of bangle unable
to mask her pulse, its quickening,

at the touch of an ordinary man—hired,
owned—surrounded by tools

of my trade and likenesses of her husband's
friends, family, looking on. Two rare mornings

in a row she dismissed her girls to market,
kneeling beside me on the stone floor,

dipping her fingers in my wetting bowl,
pressing her tiny frame against mine,

all of Egypt listening, all of Egypt
dreaming, black butterflies descending,

volcanic red bordering their wings,
arterial lace of lava shadowing her face.

Kiya

I prefer dusk, the view swimming
beneath the lotus pads—misshapen hearts—
blocking moon, sluggish carp
fleeing my hands into overcast green

of my pharaoh's pond. No-one
thinks to seek me here, except my son,
long may he outlive us all. I too soak
my feet in goat's milk, I too border

my eyes in Kohl. Yet despite my due
as First Wife, Nefertiti culls the crowd.
They caress her litter, her likeness crowns
the temples. Let her bring forth the daughters,

and I, the sons, yoked wives, neither sisters
nor confidantes, each a shoulder bearing
weight, sun-possessed head of our
husband pivoting between us.

Nefertiti On the Astral

I did what I came to do. Dead, I have the luxury
to know: the locus of power is not the body,

though how lovely: my daughter's daughter's
daughter, sitting beside the Nile, sun falling

on the brown half moon of her nipple, the blue-
veined tributary of her breast flooded with milk

at the wet clamp of her newborn's mouth.
I would choose it all again: those fevered bonds

of motherhood, the pharaoh's celestial gaze
when he chose me, roots of my hair copper,

eyelashes fringed with pollen from the shook
disks of sunflowers, tiny bristles from their arched

green necks embedded in my fingertips
making them ache as we raised our arms to Aten.

Shine, but not too bright, for light frightens,
we learned too late—and what frightens

threatens, and then you must start over.
I see the stream of exiting souls:

how they have choices, to braid with others
or remain discrete, no need to gather

in one mother, no work ever lost,
one moment the consort of Egypt, the next,

a murdered girl—and yet—such love of
Earth, with its miles of narrow canyons,

peach shafts of light crossing knobbed
knees of camels, the cloaked and waiting rider

holding out his hand, and long past sundown,
constellations bordering the open skull of night.

II

Mordred's Dream: A Refusal

(Mordred to his mother Morgayne)

I stand barefoot in the darkening woods.
Your horse bears down. His hooves crescent

the dirt, casting rinds of Earth on my feet
as he circles, one more animal bent

to your will. From muscled halves
of his chest, heat radiates. Your slight

boot and rim of cloak skim my cheek.
I'm no hunter, mother, nor simple quarry, nor witch

like you. Guinevere paces her battlements
at dawn when Arthur's gone, just a girl

in pale slippers like falcon hoods,
so lethal, so light. Were I to be mortally

wounded, would Avalon's ferry
halt for me? Unsmiling in your saddle

above, a planetary cold in your eyes,
you begin your fade; outlines of oak trunks

reassemble in the air your horse occupied,
the rowan fringe of your lips.

The Corridor

(Guinevere with her mother)

Let us begin with the worm,
its translucent omen,

the head of reason halved
and sent functioning to opposite ends,

neither male nor female,
blindly burrowing on.

In court we divide up duties,
crown one sex and not the other

but mother says dwell not on it,
power has many homes,

as we sidle down the corridor
between her door and mine

those few seconds maidless,
unattended, the mystical colors

of spun yarn in our hands,
a candle, and silvering ends of

her braids faint as spokes of dandelion
gone to seed, caught by wind

or better: blown by her breath
across the grasses to me, the plum

outline of her mouth, freckles
on her shoulders, scent of mead,

sandalwood and pheasant grease
in her hair from father's hands.

Totem

Arthur speaks to me of totems,
of journeying with Merlyn.

Yet no other hide feels a good fit;
his confidence wanes,

where doves of court
vanish in a jester's sleeve and I

long to be a faithful wife.
How well I know scorpions rest

between branch and bark of fallen
limbs and scent of a knight

after two day's ride in armour
on a borrowed horse, or weight

of Arthur's decisions, pressed freely
on me in the dark. My body

beneath his, he seeks my blessing
on the timing of sending his knights

to war. He rises light as milkweed
to dress. In dream, his men's lovers,

heavy with child, ply me one by one
with alms of buttercups and cream.

Veil

    (Guinevere to Melwas)

I run. His boot traps my hem.
My gown seam holds, my knees
strike ground. Bits of stable hay
stick to his soles, my palms

damp with dream. No one hears
but the servant girl who feigns
sleep to save our lives.
I retreat. Between inner

and outer walls of turret
ringed by stones I love,
my shoulders wick the chill.
Outside, wet dragon heads

of Camelot's banners
ripple east towards Arthur's ever
impending arrival, king not in,
nor his best knight. Neither would I

turn to them in blame, my heart
brimming with dandelions, tiny O
of stems beheaded, rimmed white
with a milk that stains

so dirt green when it contacts the skin
mother always knows where I've been.

Accomplice

    (Arthur to Guinevere)

Your body bled beneath his,
mind's border rinding white
like bare feet burning in snow.

Broken ribs, slight core housing heart
vanquished of breath, trust
in me, Lancelot, my men, anyone.

Fire long out, my men asleep under
willows, my mind vipered
with memories of my sister's

crime. On our wedding table
apples secret slick hoods
of future trees, maroon tears

suspended between golden hulls
meant to protect. Each dead stem
a reminder of fall from tree.

And Mordred, impossible
to hide from our people as you,
barren Queen, in grip of captor,

I in mine, hours by horseback between us
lined by the faint stars of the tracks
of birds long since taken flight.

Veil II

    (Guinevere to Lancelot)

Illusion reigns. No matter where I pray,
a barrier before my eyes, constant

but particulate like wild carrot's
lace with one dull red petal dead

center in a unified field of white,
thin green spindles anchored

by mother stem, sure to prick the handler's
palms. Only God could fail to fail—

another form of darkness, this light,
rimmed by flagstones mottled with veins

of ice, Arthur's shield no longer between
us. A cold front advances, blue

as dragonflies and the frozen river
you'll cross to bury my body beside his.

Transport

    (Lancelot to Guinevere)

I.

After you chose the veil, stain of mead
on stone: its purple ring, moon haloed

above snow like a man second-guessing his
will to live. Flood me with color, love,

just once again. What could I offer?
A threshold, a bit of land, garnet apples

for a girl with our eyes? Not the throne.
Nor protection from myself nor

intruder. Never in time
to intervene. My devotion

in shared desertion. Steward,
gladly, of your moments between.

II.

A fine rain and a few blackbirds
over the path we rode countless hours

wide enough for two steeds at tandem clip,
hemmed by our king—your bond—ahead,

servants behind, under casual cover day's
light gave us to love in plain sight.

In the vision, my horse travels without peer
or saddle. His heat warms my legs. Roots

of the trees reveal their spines in starts
and stops like lightning's blue

tendrils I cannot
halt from reaching your body first.

III.

Neither by dusk nor dawn, but midday's
glare. No secrets, no shadows.

The nuns' garland and a nightshift
adorn your freckled limbs. Your shroud

rustles with the dried heads
of the meadow weeds

you loved best and the husks of honey
bees. Two horses, though I'll ask

for three: One for my sorrow,
one for me, and one for the slight

arrow of you.

Anniversary

    (Guinevere to Melwas)

My gown dries in the sun. I wear it
again and again. You escaped

clean as a barefoot boy, bark pressing
its tributaries into your feet

as you took aim with a stash of stones
at apples in a neighboring tree. At its base

girls fill their skirts with bruised fruit,
while the lamp of your heart lures

the luna moths circling my head green
and heavy with the free gold of pollen.

What Sets Her Apart, Asks Jayne, Reading Another Guinevere Poem for me in Massachusetts

(Poet to Jayne)

The company she keeps: Arthur, his sorcerer sister,
their bastard son. Merlin. Her view of rain stippled Severn,
orchard's apples rinsed silver by dawn, the blue smoke

of burning peat. Hair framed by candleflame, cobalt
iris of eyes, flecks of cinnamon. Her position,
middle star of Orion's belt, between Arthur and Lancelot

more brothers than lovers, lure of Grail to assure
they'd abandon her for days alone in the Tower
with a rapist. The tear in the veil we share. I prefer

to stay with her those hours, brutal, chivalrous.
Easier than here where I dream of the acned face
of a soldier heaving at bottom of ancient

church in church's ancient time. To repeat
when I'm fourteen with a seventeen-year-old kid up the street.
Which sets me apart. *Be my parable, I'm teachable:*

you still had it all: husband, lover, convent.
Embroidered sleeves tip backs of your hands,
girl nested in woman like pit to peach.

WHAT SETS HER APART, II

Looking at Käthe Kollwitz, Women and Art, UC Davis

In *Raped*, trampled leaves, vines. Käthe left one bloom
intact. Black center tethers one unified petal. Viewer
stands at girl's bare feet, skirt taut over thighs, white flare

where naked breasts disintegrate under sun's sudden
path unobstructed where missing soldier stood up to run.
Girl's chin to sky, hair strands bled into ground. No reason

to believe she's dead. My boyfriend cheats on me. I fail
my final. Enroll in Women's Studies. In an unlit room,
a professor who calls herself Merline projects

thirty nine backlit circles bearing portaled flowers, winged
seams. *Sappho, Artemisia, Woolf*, Merline's husky voice,
assemble for Last Supper, as we writhe in slick, elated

revulsion. Behind her bedroom door, my twelve-year-old
daughter sleeps. Soon she will rise and enter the now
in which still exist Chicago's plates, Glastonbury's Tor.

Guinevere Braves High Noon in My Backyard

A soccer ball kicked by my son beheads statue
of angel that hides our spare key. In her lap, an ashtray
conch. Ear to ground, head next to feet, just as in rape

counselor's office I drew an x at far side of page
to mark my distance away from rapist. With
noticeable delight—at being right—she repositioned

my x beside x signifying event, pinning me once again.
Just as I pinch Guinevere by thorax, assigning meaning
to sheen and scale as if she'd agreed to float on her own

to back of my hand. Inside the trunk of the tree
of her time, barefoot, soaked in moss, striated
by centipede, yellow lichen frills my throat

while poet revises, circling but mute
as a girl made of cement, headless,
the back-furled lips of most private self in lap

for anyone to see. *What do you think of me now?* I ask.
She—I mean Guinevere—neither sanguine
nor sisterly, blurts, with evident

satisfaction, *You can't write your way
home*—as in *Let go*, take ball back to son,
follow him outside fence.

(25) Floors Up on Open Balcony in Seattle Guinevere Fails to Appear

Feet firm against plummet as when entering house (14),
in love with dark-haired boy (19): moccasins, gold cross,
jeans. Fate's acne-faced boy (17) answers door instead.

Palm fits shot-glass and rum slides pale as streetlamps
on brontosaurus stems, necks lit grey as sheen in dream
of hem of Jesus vanishing at corridor's end

crepe in fist, cinched, stained by grip, as when stepfather
stops me without regard for twins I babysit. Joe (6) on left,
Annie (6) on my right. He (45), shaking, says he thought

better of me ... *Don't you know, you were just
another notch in his belt.* He used an awl
to poke holes for each girl he raped. What you thought

hurt more than what went down on dirty bedspread,
faking sick to skip school, *Please don't tell
my mother.* In the embryonic forest of pre-incident

brain, there's a version in which girls choose when,
where—hear me Jesus, Guinevere, God—I promise
(this time) I won't lust for a man while I'm still just a child.

Guinevere Sets the Record Straight

    (Guinevere speaking)

Chivalry, as *you* know it, was in effect dead
before it began: draughty castles, mite laden
underwear, cows and their shepherds mired

knee deep in marsh fog, girls churning butter
in cellars for hours. You are asking
who balances the ledger. Neither

of us. Or both of us. Like the riddle
between the runes on either side of Excalibur
you must *take me up* and *cast me away*.

Stop hiding from the rest of your life
by trying to understand mine. Burn blue,
undefiled, amid the asters of the stars.

GUINEVERE, 4:33 AM, SAN DIEGO, CALIFORNIA

(Guinevere speaking)

I am the White Rose of Glastonbury. Write that down,
she insists, leaning over me. *It's so obvious,*

I say, *in drawings we still do of your people: phallus
of knight in helmet, cloaked girl on forest floor,*

*pleasure button of her slender hooded frame. Tell Arthur
I'm done.* She says, *I think that's my line.* I reply,

*Let's send the three crones standing guard over his body
back in time to spring you of the grip of Melwas.*

She shakes her head. *You are obsessed. It's done.
Over.* Goes on instead about the fertile sage furrows

of fog surrounding the Tower the fortnight she was captive,
leylines of the saints crossing beneath her feet so potent

her head ached as if struck. *I am,* she repeats, *the White
Rose of Glastonbury. You will write that down?* Later,

I'll divine what she means: sometimes you have to sacrifice
a blossom to the sovereign in winter for the right to bloom.

I succumb to the life I live, my century, my bed,
angling sideways between third child, Siberian

Husky, and cat, soles of my husband's feet hot
cupping mine. *I'll be back*, she promises. *I bet*,

I say, *in couplets*, and she smiles, though
for the first time the outlines of her dress blur

like milkweed tufts loosed from grip of pod.

III

III

Someone

visits my body by night.
In a parallel world of dream,

I see a red pearl
and a cardinal, flying,

then still, in branches
of the orange tree.

Through tears, a red king,
some ancient enemy,

hurling down the black stem
of the glassblower's lance

with the mouth
of an apprentice. I wake

while you dissemble above me,
a chrysalis of white veins

in the amber dawn.
The cries of the first birds

melt in our untouching mouths.

Peer Counselor

It was my fault. I took a drink, angels offer
no velvet cure, nor peaches in their laps for me

nor girlhood span of years to doubt their choices
at the crosshairs of one chronic location. Barefoot

in a shabby chair in a borrowed office on campus
she lets me finish the rehearsed poem of blame, numb

veil down arm, the quiet *no* to acned chin approaching
mine, the instant assessment of his intent and the decision

not to feel. Angels tuck like every doe, their necessary
hooves beneath themselves, fur side facing fawn

to better rest in shade of tree. But I'm no fawn, this girl
too young to be my mother. Beyond cracked door a man

in tool belt gripping toolbox enters without knocking.
Of my stiffening she apologizes, He's here to fix the copier.

His back to us, he does his job while she resumes
hers, folds her legs, grasps her ankles

leans towards me, her little voice encircling us both
like a cocoon or some indigo dusk's moon ring or crystal

astral pod feathered white like Midwest windows in winter
in which I could suddenly see the holographic self

portioned out like a broken mirror held loosely in its frame
There were two of you with bodies in the room—

Which one of you chose to enter yours by force?

Dragonfly

In lieu of the ring, a carbon fiber frame.
You had it custom done, turned it for me
in the sun outside our one-room flat,
this way: violet green, that: honey red.
First ride: a pair of shag-lumped llamas,
a kestrel on the wire, a sheep and two lambs
you never saw. Twenty-three miles of hairpin curves
above Cazadero: staring down the cleft of muscle
in your calves, clinging to the promise of the descent
down Meyer's Grade, blocking out the downshifting
gear directives streaming from your mouth. Summit's
view: redwoods to pastures to ocean cliffs
where you stopped for water,
long enough to hear me wonder aloud:
what did I do to you one life back?
We laughed, agreed: *I* was the rider.
This time around, I'll try my hand
at raising the children, and you,
slow enough to see the kestrel,
color of the sky, me.

Absolute Power

    (after the movie by same title)

Eastwood, as robber, in shadows
trapped watching Hackman, as president

methodically beating the mistress to death.
I ask them to turn it down—my husband,

his mother—watching TV in the next room
as cramping swarms the dromedary

hump of my frame, dull cudgels of first
contractions and the boxcar blinks

of the seconds of rest to tolerate
alone, an hour that repeats for thirty-six,

so much harder to bear than a few stabs
that afternoon years ago, the minimal

blood, the acned face of a stranger re-clasping
his belt, the things I told myself to calm

down at fourteen. How dare the old trespass
trespass now, unable like other good mothers

to birth without epidural—the relentless
rhythm of pain fissuring the halves of my

brain—how could I stay, give in,
allow it to repeat and nowhere like then

to run. But at last they placed her,
tiny, hot, against my breast, my life

mine again. Bless the robber, bless
the president, the mistress on her way

to heaven, the three days of crushing
my husband's hands while he counted

me home, the streets we drove to get here
and back, the egrets in the meridian—the grid

of the city—everything—suffused
with a light I no longer refused to see.

Third Planet from the Sun

On the way to the hospital, a car upside down in the ditch.
Antlered globes of mistletoe nutted the oak trees;

flying at right angles to the windshield, egrets: cotton.
Then, waiting for doctor to finish stitching,

our son's wrinkled fist gripping your thumb,
heatlamp warming you both, no thought

of chrysalis or poetry, placental dendrites
a-roil in a silver tureen, waiting for door to shut,

before visitors, flowers, the thousand moments
to follow raising this newborn—who'll out us,

our flaws, like mist garneting a spider's web;
we're light, green—as cabbage spines nested—

our hollow-veined wings hardening in the sun.

Orion

He takes more than milk by morning.
If I close my eyes against the suck and thrush

of his purple tongue there's a chance the dream
will linger, or that former self who lived

seven years solo in Iowa before I married,
then gave birth three times. Who is that girl

with time to burn sandalwood—ticking
pilot light on a white gas stove—the plush

rush of blue flame morning of first snow,
heartwood lit, sending up

its trills of scent and silver fudgling rings—
Oh bless the trees of the genus Santalum.

For now I'm barely caged in a collapsible form
like the diamond grill inside an elevator box

I once rode in Paris just wide enough for me
and one suitcase. It's how we're meant to arrive

on Earth but somehow it seems we come with more—
leftover notions of the lives before like a dancing

hangover—the smell of strangers' cigarettes
in your hair, the foam wreaths of their beer

webbing your toes. But what's essential is here—
my breast, my body's milk, his mouth,

two heartbeats, and the thrumming of blood:
You again, you again.

November Butterfly

It's easy to love the sun
and the roses it fires,
blood cardinals
flying over snow,
three black horses
running midmorning
in the rain,
a blue heron
on a downed tree
in river's mist.

But what of tar fissures
on backroads off the grid,
a liver sheened reptile
clambering out of the ditch,
cold-rimmed hubcaps,
headlights, a voice
two states away on the radio,
a butterfly with a frayed
wing pinned living
to the windshield.

It's easy to love some women,
emanating green, moonskinned,
quiet, enchanting,
as sunlight
through undersides of leaves.

Winter in the thighs,
we hibernate in rooms they've left,
and pray they'll return, notice us,
or let fall
some butter from their palms.

I wish I were a flower,
or the maker,
to mend you.
I held out my finger—
not a stick—
and up you grappled,
unfurled a tunneled up
tongue,
for one last taste,
or to ward me off.

So easy to muck the translation
no common language—
that gap between the self one loves
and the self one fears.
I can't fill out your wing,
but I can look you
in the unblinking amber screen
of your eye,

and set you on this leaf.

The Longing of the Species

You've talked me into this—
(much forgotten bridge)

children in the house.
No seatbelts. A peppermint loose

of its crinkle, red-gold light
of a blown nova in the mirror,

last bead of pull-string
notched fast. The filament floods—

you want to see. I want to sleep,
drift nested like this in the Horsehead

Nebula of Orion's belt. A memory
—not mine—rushes along my spine:

her face, outlined sediment grey
like a trilobite in a museum fossilized

by all that came to die on top of it.
I'll let her go if you stay. Give over

your last, slight as spheres
of dew on flute-tips of clover.

OCELLI

Just married then, and a child sucking milk
from coconut cap of my brain, shins weak,

eye sockets dry, disturbed by the husband's
seeming freedoms, males wickedly pretty

even after the camouflage of marriage, dreaming
of water, soldiers, and the giant owl butterflies

of Central America circling banana plantations
at dusk and dawn, wings ringed with ocelli

in surmised mimicry of owls' sets of eyes
—unless wrong—the naturalists—paired

or single, in lab or field, guessing about lust,
tracking its path erroneously like me:

Blue Morpho flashing of my husband
on the astral, electric blue then black shadow

of folded wings through waterfall
and back, through dappled light disappearing,

confusing predators, losing wives. Surely those eyes
persist from the time before fruit or promise

of ownership by vow, from miles of planetless space
between incarnation, when I was sleek, as round,

but hollow, quill of soul stripped free of wing
and the obsession to fly.

God's in the Butter

and the cool pull of household order;
in the soft spot: thumbprint's worth of skin

dented heartward, pulsing over the open star
between the four quarters of my daughter's skull;

in the silver water sifting from the whipping cream,
and in the fluff of duck feather my brother

fluffed against his nose, sucking his thumb
nights my mother worked;

in the voice of the woman crying at the coffee shop
holding hands with the father of her infant son

listening to him list reasons he won't come home to them,
and in the hardness day after day, getting along

with the father of my children;
in the glittering orbs one needs gloves to handle:

mothballs dropped under floorboards for warding off
winter's opossums, and in the chilled

beaters, cream coated, one for you and one for me,
best raw, no need for sugar or vanilla.

Kiss me: staying with you or anyone
depends on this tasting God in everything.

A Maritime Trilogy

I. *Querent*

Dead girls' dolls line the sills,
antique ruffles of their petticoats

stitched a century back; carpet
beetles seed the batting, cat

curled in a crib. Money paid,
cards skim one by one

across the oval glass table
above Madame's tassled lap:

This ten of swords represents you.
Crossing you, on horseback,

this knight, red haired, pale of face.
You desire a child by him.

I fidget, riveted by the row of blades
buried in one spine. She hesitates.

I miss my father, who warned
not to touch the monarch's wing,

so I hid my fingers, already heavened
with amber cinnamon.

II. *Seer*

These girls strike me green. Their mothers
fail them. I'd rather this querent hadn't
come. I'll keep my seer's oath, not disclose
how brief her life's duration appears.

Or have I erred, overlaid,
as lesser clairvoyants do, my future
over hers. Best return cards
to cinched safety of silk

and walk ocean's rim
where hinged cobalt horns
gull-grey and slick with oysters cling
to wave wet rocks offshore

where an outcast once rowed
towards a naked girl and her sister,
honey dripping through holes
of abalone shells onto their wrists,

instinct's irritant warning
gemmed, then ignored, dull
as land girls they were the moment
he advanced, olive bands of kelp

trailing their own uprooted bulbs,
each head beery brown and hollow.

III. *Selke*

Taste the water before you step in.
Strip your waist of its summer heat.

No need to complain of stolen
skin and fractured identities.

If you wake beside a man
you were half the choosing

just as at birth your mother's
devotion to you doubled, her

omens halving in your newborn
frame. Take a sister with you. One

of you will see more clearly than the other.
In every family, at least one breaks

free. Come, bring your mouth to mine.

Black Angel: Scripted, Never Shot

>   (Oakland Cemetery, Iowa City, Iowa)

Two: sisters, pasts, and halves
of a just-cut pomegranate.
Close up of red wicking into snow

ribbing angel's hem.
Splice in the Iowa River by night.
Globed lamps of path

on black stems, juxtaposed with columns
linking student studios to Art Museum.
Face her. Take her hands in yours. Spin

weaving the span of pillars, identical
raw cotton skirts beveling against bare shins,
then close up of v of fingers

interlocking without interruption,
centrifugal motion
of two fused beings

against black backdrop,
a persistence of the continuum of whites:
Perseid meteors

of late July too fine to catch on film
at the crossroads of their slimming
disappearing as they arrive.

Wind God, Ghost Ranch

You appear in pattern of wood
on my bathroom door behind towel

on its hook. Foot, rind of heel, O
of oracle's mouth, pale pine growth rings

in mimicry, and above, male outlines
of bushy brows. Two halves fractionally

misaligned by the carpenter, psychic
snapshot of the dissembling that occurs

after body's forced apart at yoni line.
Just as two halves of a broken plate

make a matching scar. Press tight, scar
disappears. How you think of yourself, or

can't after. Unlike body's chiral twins: hands,
feet, a pair of empty gloves. You were there

as I rinsed blood from thighs,
little brother begging from far side

of door to be let in, when I bound him
to keep and carry my secret, doubling the pain.

I should've given it to you instead,
you with dirty snout, elf-ears, teeth bared.

DIVORCE, OR THE YEAR OF 11 HOUSES

We met and fought by chance one last time
in the produce aisle after you chose Dad,
our sister and I chose Mom. I stood in the false

rain pleading for you to turn, as the tiny squall
made its way down the banks of tomatoes and ice-berg
lettuce, misting from hidden nozzles to rumble

of a thunder invoking Illinois, where we at least
had one another and summer crickets by night,
a pretend circus of box springs and sheets,

tickets we drew by hand, knee to knee
in the Valient, or backseat of a three wheel bicycle
our father steered, bows and arrows balanced

between our knees. By winter, cross-legged
in red domes of our flying saucers skimming
snow, outline of our breaths—crossing as we spun—

as visible as your biceps of now, your bleached
hair, your retreating back. You're in love
and won't be coming home. Years later

in a basement over ping pong, your daughter
toddling past, you say *I'm sorry I couldn't bear
knowing about the rape* and I say

I'm sorry I asked you to keep it a secret,
no stalemate of blame enough time
can't erase, the relief of the focus of tiny white

ball to return, the short and crossable net between,
table—on wheels—so easily folded
and set aside at game's end.

A Boy Like You

I know you're home—there's a GI Joe head
in my sink; I'll find a burned butter knife

in the trash, man doll's nose salvaged,
melted back from some planned park-yard

tragedy or dog attack staged by a boy
like you. Computer's on, you

buy and sell your damaged Joes.
It's 2 a.m., I'm on my knees

cutting up National Geographics,
good books, last year's calendars,

pasting fourteen-year-old girls into the middle
of the Nile, Saturn's rings,

or Hamlet's soliloquy, anywhere
she can escape the childhood

rapist. You undress, dress,
Joes like those you left behind

in Ireland the summer your parents
divorced. You never

got to say goodbye to friends,
the room of toys your father

shipped stateside one year later.
The hurt's slow to leave us both,

but pour me a cup of tea.
This weekend, take me, the kids,

to the sea. I trust you
like a brother. Better—you've

won my heart: you're safe enough
to take to bed. There'll be time

again to lie in the sun,
and desire come home to me.

3 A.M. Service, New Melleray Monastery

Blood berries of our taillights
in the Iowa snow. Orion in the sky.
Brother Felix signs us in. Stale cookies
from the basement jar, a bitter sip
of Orange Pekoe tea. A narrow bed
with tan coverlet. One casement

overlooking the courtyard
and dark of the monks' wing.
One candle, ladder stranded,
on the stone wall facing us.
Higher yet, an open window,
wide enough for a fistful of snow

or an owl. It's the time of night
I was born; the brothers file out,
leaving the candle lit. A hot shower later,
it's naked to sleep, like the Lady
of Guadalupe, skin red as her satin,
the green air above the bed sifting

over my shoulders, sheets poked gold
with stars, prayers, a rind of the moon,
and the up-stretched hands of some androgyne
cherub cupping my feet. It'll go, slow,
after childbirth, my second, this gripping—
like a child urged against her gut by an adult

to hold a stranger's rabbit,
white fur thinner than milkweed silk.
That panicked mile of open prairie
in one shock-jerk kick, scratch marks
welling down one's arm. God's nothing
like that, but is instead the voice that told you

not to hold the rabbit, the heat
in the sea-star nub of one's nipple
down the newborn's throat, and the blind,
dead-sure rooting of my son
rolling towards the spot in our bed
I've risen from to write this poem.

Acknowledgements

I am grateful for the daily support of my writing flock, the Diamond Flamingos: Jayne Benjulian, Sandra Hunter, Marcia Meier, Lisa Rizzo, Barbara Rockman, Ruth Thompson, Michelle Wing and Barbara Ann Yoder.

Four lifelong writing companions, Mary Allen, Liz Brennan, Patricia Hall, and Penina Taesali, are also due gratitude, as are photographer Robyn Beattie, sculptor Sandy Frank, and Sydney Griffin.

Two indispensable individuals who fed and watered me with copious pots of tea and coffee, whose love and humor bolstered my ability to complete this project: Lydia Stewart and Jerilynn Wagner. And Aunt Rose: for leading me to Persia.

I wish to also thank Elizabeth Schreiber for listening and for her profound kindness that initiated transformation during a time of formidable duress.

Supporting organizations and structures include A Room of Her Own Foundation, *She Writes*, and *Mother Writer Mentor*.

I am also indebted to the ongoing collaborative partnership I share with writer and fellow editor at *The Fertile Source* and *MWM*, Jessica Powers.

Thank you to the editors of the following venues:

The Art of Bicycling: A Treasury of Poems ("Dragonfly")

Blood Orange Review ("Sylvia, Section II," "3 a.m. New Melleray Monastery")

Chaparral ("Peer Counselor")

The Dickens, Winner of the Eugene Ruggles Award ("God's in the Butter," "November Butterfly")

Holding on and Letting Go: Anthology of Coe College Writers ("Someone")

Kalliope, Finalist for the Sue Saniel Elkind National Poetry Award ("Chanter's Daughter")

NonBinary Review ("Thumbelina")

Poetry Flash ("Mordred's Dream")

Prairie Wolf Press ("Nefertiti on the Astral")

Salome Magazine ("Marilyn," "She Dressed in a Hurry")

Soundings East, Runner-up for the Claire Keyes Poetry Award ("Black Angel: Scripted, Never Shot")

Spoon River Poetry Review, Honorable Mention, Editor's Prize ("For the Love of Three Oranges")

Stone Canoe Online ("Ophelia," "Nefertiti Among Us")

V's place, blog ("Amelia")

Poems in Section II about Guinevere draw on inspiration from Marion Zimmer Bradley's *The Mists of Avalon*, Dion Fortune's *Glastonbury: Avalon of the Heart*, Malory's *Morte d'Arthur*, Mary Stewart's *The Crystal Cave*, Persia Woolley's *The Guinevere Trilogy*, and T.H. White's *The Once and Future King*.

ABOUT TANIA PRYPUTNIEWICZ

A graduate of the Iowa Writers' Workshop, Tania Pryputniewicz is the Managing Poetry Editor at The Fertile Source (www.fertilesource.com) and co-founder of Mother, Writer, Mentor (www.motherwritermentor.com).

She teaches workshops including Transformative Blogging, Poetry Forms, Poetry of Motherhood, Poetry of Fatherhood, and Exploring the Minor Mentors of Tarot. She blogs at Feral Mom, Feral Writer (www.poetrymom.blogspot.com) and lives in San Diego, California with her husband, three children, blue-eyed Siberian Husky and two tubby housecats with identical sets of stripes.

Her award-winning micro movies feature poetry paired with the photography of Robyn Beattie and the music of Stephen Pryputniewicz. *She Dressed in a Hurry (for Lady Diana)*, *Amelia*, *Nefertiti Among Us*, *Nefertiti on the Astral*, *Corridor*, *Mordred's Dream*, *Thumbelina*, and *The Three Oranges* may be viewed at her main website: (www.taniapryputniewicz.com).

www.ingramcontent.com/pod-product-compliance
Lightning Source LLC
Chambersburg PA
CBHW032046290426
44110CB00012B/980